Helping Habitats

Barbara L. Webb

ROURKE PUBLISHING

www.rourkepublishing.com

www.rourkepublishing.com

PHOTO CREDITS: Cover: © deetone, John Saunders; Title Page, 4, 5: © Josef Friedhuber; Page 6, 7: © Eduardo Mariano Rivero; Page 8, 9: © Nils Kahle; Page 10: © Dawn Nichols; Page 11: © SZE FEI WONG, Didier Brandelet; Page 12: © Peregrine; Page 12, 13: © Jinlide; Page 15: © Christopher Futcher; Page 14: © RelaxFoto.de; Page 16: © Mayumi Terao; Page 17: © Thomas Lozinski; Page 18: © Krzysztof Odziomek; Page 19: © Mr-Eckhart; Page 21: © Patrick Herrera, Michael DeLeon, Jonathan Ross; Page 22: © Mykola Velychko;

Edited by Meg Greve

Cover and Interior design by Tara Raymo

Library of Congress Cataloging-in-Publication Data

Webb, Barbara L.
Helping Habitats / Barbara L. Webb.
    p. cm. -- (Green Earth Science Discovery Library)
Includes bibliographical references and index.
ISBN 978-1-61741-770-2 (hard cover) (alk. paper)
ISBN 978-1-61741-972-0 (soft cover)
Library of Congress Control Number: 2011924816

Rourke Publishing
Printed in the United States of America, North Mankato, Minnesota
060711
060711CL

www.rourkepublishing.com - rourke@rourkepublishing.com
Post Office Box 643328 Vero Beach, Florida 32964

Table of Contents

Animals Need Habitats

All over the world, animals live in **habitats**. Animals survive by **adapting** to the kinds of food, shelter, and weather in their habitats.

Fun Fact:

Polar bears have rough pads on their feet to keep them from slipping.

Polar bears are adapted to the cold North Pole, where they walk on chunks of ice to hunt seals for food.

Toucans are adapted
to eating fruit that grows in
the rainforest.

Figs

Guava

Fun Fact:
If a toucan gets too hot, its body sends extra heat into its large bill.

Parrot fish are adapted to eating the seaweed that grows in their **coral reef** habitat.

Seaweed

Habitats in Danger

The Arctic

Some animal habitats are changing or disappearing.

Rainforest

Coral Reef

This is bad news for animals. It is hard for animals to adapt and survive if their habitats change too quickly.

Humans Hurt and Help Habitats

Humans are hurting some animal habitats with their choices. It is not too late to help.

People cut down big areas of forest habitat to sell trees or make room for farms.

Greater Adjutant Stork

13

Burning coal to make electricity makes **greenhouse gases**, which warm up the Earth and melt the **polar** ice.

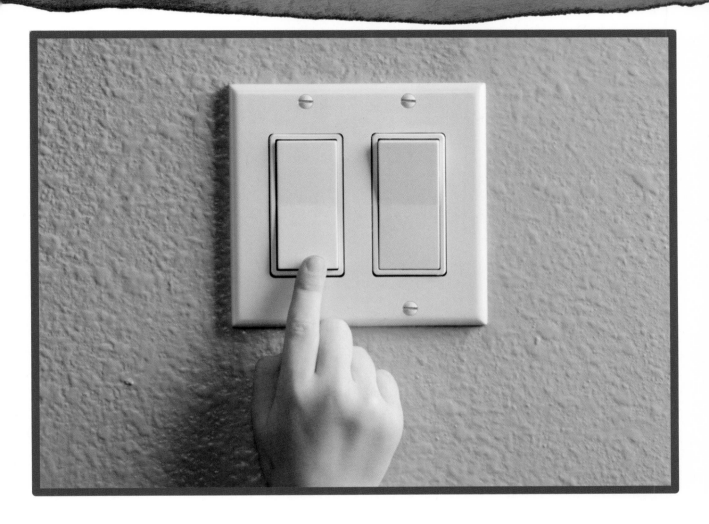

We can help by turning off the lights when we leave a room.

Cutting down old rainforest trees to make furniture shrinks the toucan's habitat.

We can help by building furniture with fast-growing materials like **bamboo**.

Catching too many parrot fish upsets the coral reef.

Tip:

If you are swimming in the ocean, remember to SOS, which means stand on sand, *not on coral. This rule protects the little coral animals from human feet.*

We can help by making laws against **overfishing**.

You Can Help Habitats

What can you do?

- Unplug your computer and games when you are not using them.

- Ask where your food comes from.

- Read and learn more about science.

When you do these things, you are helping habitats!

Try This

Whether you live in the city, suburb, or country, you can create a habitat for animals. Here are some ideas:

• Plant flowers that will attract bees, butterflies, and hummingbirds in a garden or pot. Butterfly bush, purple coneflower, and bee balm are all easy to grow from seeds.

• If you have a backyard, put some rocks and a shallow dish of water in a shady spot. Turn a clay pot upside down in your habitat and prop open one side with a stone to make a door. Wait for toads to move in!

• Ask a parent if they will save branches from tree trimming. Put the branches, some dead leaves, and rocks in a corner of your yard to create a habitat for birds, turtles, and small animals.

Glossary

adapting (uh-DAPT-ing): changing to be able to eat a certain food or live in a certain place in order to survive

bamboo (bam-BOO): a plant in the grass family with thick stems that can be used like tree wood

coral reef (KOR-uhl reef): a structure, usually found in shallow ocean water, made out of the skeletons of tiny animals called corals

greenhouse gases (GREEN-houss GASS-uhz): gases like carbon dioxide that trap heat in the Earth's atmosphere

habitats (HAB-uh-tats): places in nature where plants and animals live

overfishing (OH-vur-FISH-ing): the act of catching a number of fish that harms a fish population or a habitat

polar (POH-lur): having to do with the cold and icy regions of the North or South Poles of the Earth

Index

Websites

www.pbskids.org/shareastory/stories/64/index.html

www.clean-air-kids.org.uk/globalwarming.html

www.kidsforsavingearth.org/index.html

About the Author

Barbara Webb spends each summer creating a city habitat for bees, butterflies, and birds on her roof deck in Chicago. She has written five green science books for kids.